# Without a Trace

**Shirley Baker**

# Without a Trace

## Manchester and Salford in the 1960s

The History Press

First published 2018
Reprinted 2019, 2020

The History Press
97 St George's Place,
Cheltenham, GL50 3QB
www.thehistorypress.co.uk

British Library Cataloguing in Publication Data.
A catalogue record for this book is available from the British Library.

ISBN 978 0 7509 8898 8

Typesetting and origination by The History Press
Printed by Imak, Turkey

# Foreword

The photographs of Shirley Baker (1932–2014) capture the recent history of inner-city Salford and Manchester. This body of work, created over a twenty-year period, came to define her distinctive vision. The demolition of whole streets of Victorian terraced houses in the 1960s and 70s radically reshaped the landscape and communities of Salford, Manchester and many other northern cities; and Baker created artistic images inspired by the human stories of the communities that lived amidst this urban destruction before they were re-housed.

It is Baker's focus on how these clearances affected the individuals and communities that lived there that makes her work so popular. The recent Shirley Baker exhibition, *Women and Children; and Loitering Men* at Manchester Art Gallery was always full of visitors and much praised by the public and critics alike, winning the City Life Best Exhibition of 2017. Many people who had lived through that period as children (including some who appear in the photographs) came to see the exhibition and spoke of their happy childhoods and the freedom afforded to them.

Baker's work is more than documentation of social history – she had a strong artistic agenda. She captured the poetry in everyday human interactions through carefully composed compositions, which appear natural and spontaneous. She was a compassionate and humorous teller of stories that portray the spectrum of human resilience. Baker depicted the day-to-day lives of working communities and made the everyday appear momentarily extraordinary.

Shirley Baker was a pioneer – both as a woman and as one of the very few British street photographers to work in colour in post-war Britain. The results, created in 1965 but unpublished until recently, reveal her artistic response to the medium, particularly to the reds, blues, greens and yellows of the Kodachrome film. They feature her characteristic empathy and lack of moralising, while the addition of colour enriches the subject matter and locations, and they can be seen as a symbol of life and optimism, of hope and pleasure, in what might otherwise be seen as bleak urban environments.

Shirley Baker is thought to be the only woman to practice street photography in Britain during the post-war era, yet her work was recognised relatively late in her fifty-five-year career and is only now receiving a second wave of appreciation since her death. I am delighted that this publication will reassert her relevance and talent and disseminate her work to a new generation.

*Natasha Howes, Senior Curator, Manchester Art Gallery*

# Shirley Baker

## Photographer and Writer

Shirley Baker (1932–2014) was one of the most prominent female twentieth-century British social documentary photographers. She is best known for the post-war inner-city street photographs of Manchester and Salford featured in this book. Her wanderings also produced many more stunning collections, including the glamorous life of the South of France and the fashion-concious inhabitants of Camden Town and Oxford Street, London.

The combination of Shirley's northern roots and her curiosity and engagement with people resulted in some emotively powerful images of working-class communities during the 1960s slum clearances. Her work is sensitive, yet unsentimental, with humour evident in many of her photographs. She preferred to work in black and white, but experimented in the summer of 1965 with her first collection of colour photography.

Born in Kersal, north Salford, she grew up in Manchester with her identical twin sister. Her father was a furniture maker and her mother a milliner. She married a doctor and went on to live in Wilmslow, Cheshire, with her husband and daughter.

An uncle gave her and her sister a Brownie box camera each when they were just eight years old. Her sister soon discarded it, but Shirley never put hers down. She was thrilled when she successfully developed her first black and white film in the darkness of the coal shed.

With her new-found passion for the camera and her artistic eye it made sense for Shirley to study Pure Photography at Manchester College of Technology. She was

one of a small number of women in post-war Britain to receive formal photographic training. Shirley went on to take further courses in photography at London Regent Street Polytechnic, London College of Printing and the University of Derby.

Shirley started work as an industrial photographer and went on to become a lecturer at Salford College of Art and Manchester Polytechnic. Ideally, she would have liked to have become a press photographer for the *Guardian*, but as a female photographer in a male-dominated profession, Union restrictions meant that she was unable to get the necessary press card. Instead she went freelance, working as a photographer and writer for a variety of magazines and newspapers. She also undertook a number of special projects: one at the Royal Manchester Children's Hospital and another a commission for Manchester Airport. It was freelancing that she preferred because she could set her own projects and be her own boss. She particularly admired the work of Cartier-Bresson for his slice-of-life pictures.

Shirley's early street photographs were taken with Super Ikonta and Rolleiflex cameras with 120-size film. She went on to work with 35mm film with Leica, Contax, Minolta and tiny half-frame Pen cameras. She started with standard lenses, but later converted to zoom for focal length. For her colour images, she used Kodachrome 64 film.

Shirley published two books in her lifetime, which are now collectors' items. Throughout her career her photographs were exhibited widely throughout the North-west of England and in group exhibitions in Sao Paolo and Paris. She had discussed the idea of her first solo exhibition in London with The Photographers' Gallery and in 2015, a year after her sudden death, the London Gallery held a major exhibition of her work titled 'Women and Children; and Loitering Men' with an accompanying publication. This exhibition toured for three years to Hong Kong, Shenzhen, Madrid and Manchester. Her work has since been shown in group exhibitions by Burberry, Open Eye and Somerset House. Her solo exhibition 'On the Beach' is still on tour.

*Nan Levy, daughter of Shirley Baker*

# Introduction

Shirley started to photograph the streets of Manchester and Salford in the early 1960s when homes were being demolished and communities were being uprooted. Perceptively, she felt a massive historical and sociological event about to happen on her doorstep – and took her cameras into action to capture what would soon be a bygone age. 'Whole streets were disappearing, and I hoped to capture some trace of everyday life of the people who lived there. I was particularly interested in the more mundane, even trivial, aspects of life that were not being recorded by anyone else.'

Shirley's powerful images show small slices of everyday life that each tell a story. Children play in the streets without fear, often with toy guns that concern parents today. A wrecked car is something wonderful to play in, and women hang the washing across the cobbled streets where traffic is a rarity. The elderly watch the children as they play. Wealth is absent, but community spirity is there in rich abundance.

Her curiosity and fine camerawork recorded people and communities involved in fundamental change. Before people's homes were demolished as part of the huge slum clearance programme, Shirley was able to capture some of the street life as it had been for generations before the change. The old smokestack industries and textile mills were either demolished or converted for fresh use. The old Manchester docks were transformed into what is now Salford Quays. The regenerated dockland is now full of glittering office blocks, modern apartments, restaurants and the splendid Lowry building with its art galleries, theatres and leisure areas. It is hard to

believe that this was once the thriving port of Manchester (the fourth largest port in the UK).

Salford had some of the worst housing in the country, with much of its housing development dating back to the Industrial Revolution. Subgrade dwellings had been built very closely together with factories and workshops sandwiched between. After the war, the city council planned to redevelop the area aiming for a better environment. As sites were cleared, tower blocks were built to rehouse the communities. There were spaces for parks, a library, banks and shopping precincts. The demolition was very slow, the area was dirty and derelict and extremely noisy. Some of the photographs show the spaces where buildings had been demolished and others show the new replacement tower blocks looming behind the remaining houses like aliens.

By 1965 there were plans for a slum clearance drive to demolish the remaining 54,000 houses in ten years. The dilapidated houses were marked with an X for demolition. These condemned houses were damp and cold, with no heating or hot water, no bath or inside toilet. Many had leaking roofs, mouldy walls and peeling paint. People were living in extremely harsh conditions. Many families and single parents were unaware of their social security benefit entitlement and were struggling to put food on the table. 'My sympathies lie with the people who were forced to exist miserably, often for months on end – sometimes years – whilst demolition went on all around them.'

Some of the people who had been rehoused in new flats felt as if they had been transported to paradise; yet others resented having to leave their homes, families and friends. The communities were being broken up and many people did not understand the reason for the change. Some refused to go to the new places that were offered to them by the council. 'My interest grew into a compulsion even though the notion of someone wandering the un-picturesque streets of Manchester and Salford with a camera seemed quite crazy to most people then.' Shirley was compelled to revisit the streets time and time again to observe and record the everyday world around her, managing to capture the character of the way of life in the afternoon light, before all the streets had been totally demolished. Her pictures capture the moment.

Pets were not allowed in the new council flats. This did not help relations between the council and the people. Dogs and cats were abandoned by their owners and they were seen roaming the streets, looking for scraps put out by sympathetic neighbours who had not yet been evicted.

The air was thick with smoke from the fires and dust from the crumbling brickwork, which crashed to the ground. As the roof slates were removed, they were slid down planks and dumped with other rubbish into the backs of lorries. This made for constant noise throughout the day. Unwanted furniture and wrecked cars littered the open spaces. All of this devastation bore a close resemblance to a bombsite. Shirley was fascinated by how the textures and abstract patterns of the peeling facade of the old houses changed over time.

'The children would often clamber all over me when they spotted the camera, begging me to take their picture.' Shirley never posed her pictures, but often the children would pose themselves. Children would enjoy playing in the streets whilst their mothers were chatting. Shirley felt comfortable amongst the people as she wandered the streets, observing their everyday life. 'Eventually most people relaxed and seemed to forget that I was there at all.' She noticed toddlers and babies were often left with older children during the day while their parents were at work and some very young children were spotted wandering the streets without any apparent supervision. The children saw the 'bombsite' as a huge adventure playground and enjoyed climbing and playing and rummaging for hidden treasure amongst the abandoned cars and rubble.

Just a couple of streets away there were rows of houses that were not due for immediate demolition: these were extremely well kept, with lace curtains and ornaments visible through the sparklingly clean windows. The front of the houseS were pristine. Some householders, nervous of vandalism, would put notices in their front window to say that their house was still occupied.

The old streets are no longer there, and the people have been moved. The areas have been redeveloped to form a new and totally different environment. As Shirley once said, 'Photographs miraculously preserve traces of the light which illuminates the present, and although the images represent just fragments of the life of Manchester and Salford seen through my eyes and the eye of my camera, they are shared experiences. I hope by bridging time through the magic of photography, a connection has been made with a past that should not be forgotten.'

Rows of terraced houses were flattened, leaving just the pub, the corner shop and the doctor's surgery still standing. These were always the last to go. As evicted families moved out, the squatters and vagrants moved in for a few nights' shelter. Neighbouring children would have fun smashing every windowpane to smithereens – vandalism was a great pastime. Eventually, the official demolition gangs would move in with their bulldozers, swinging lead balls and axes. When the homes had finally disappeared, travelling gypsies set up camp on the empty, desolate landscapes, and their children played amongst the rubble. As the streets were vanishing, men with their carts and old prams would ravage the sites, looking for anything that could be recycled. They would take their full carts to sorting sheds where rags and metal were sorted and weighed, later to be collected by agents and sold on to rag merchants and metal dealers.

'Often when I came to a cleared site it was like standing on an empty stage; the actors had gone and there was nothing to show who they were or what the play had been about. Memories linger, but without some hint or trace of reality, they too die out and come to nothing. Perhaps these photographs will give substance to some of those memories.'

*Nan Levy, daughter of Shirley Baker*

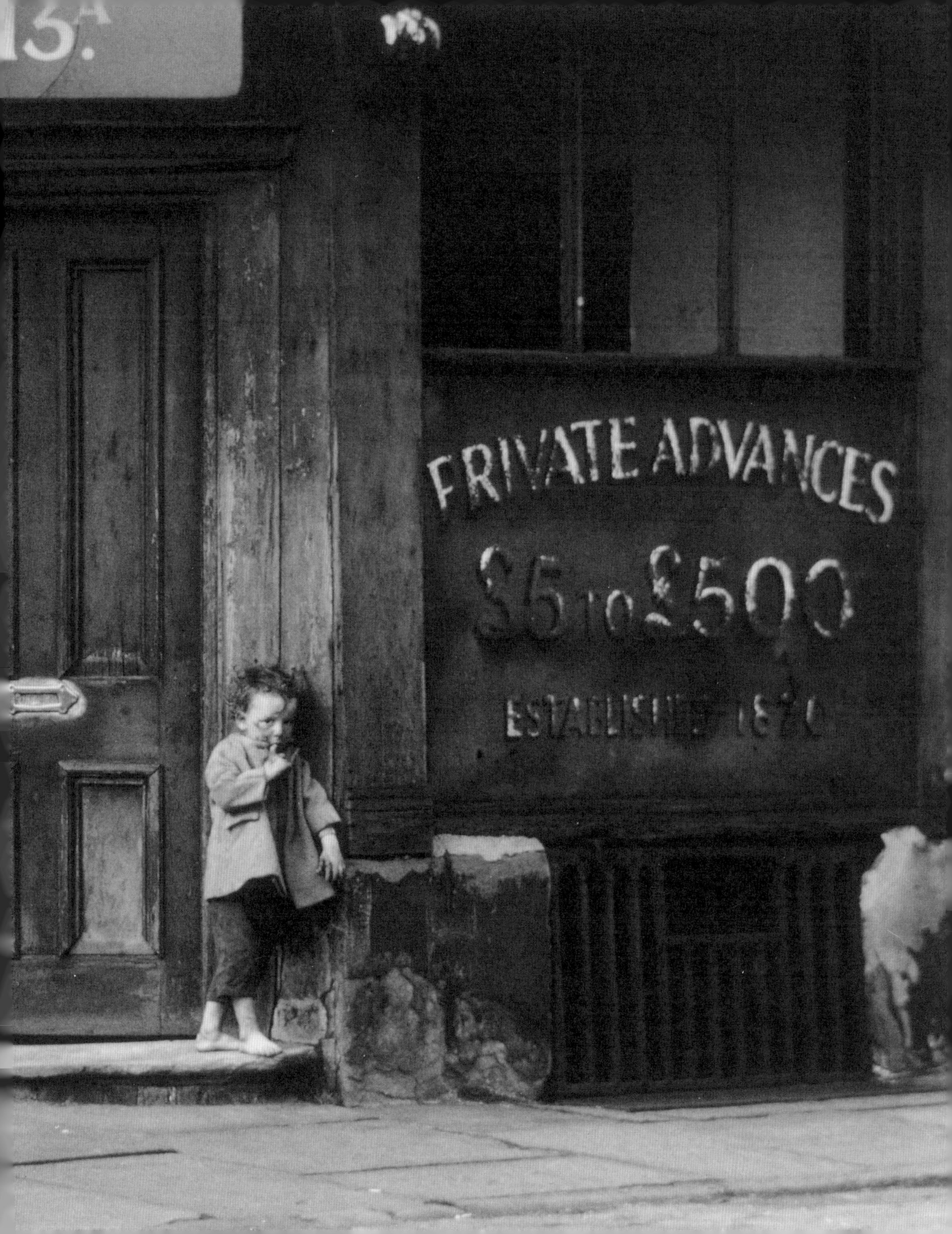
PRIVATE ADVANCES
£5 TO £500

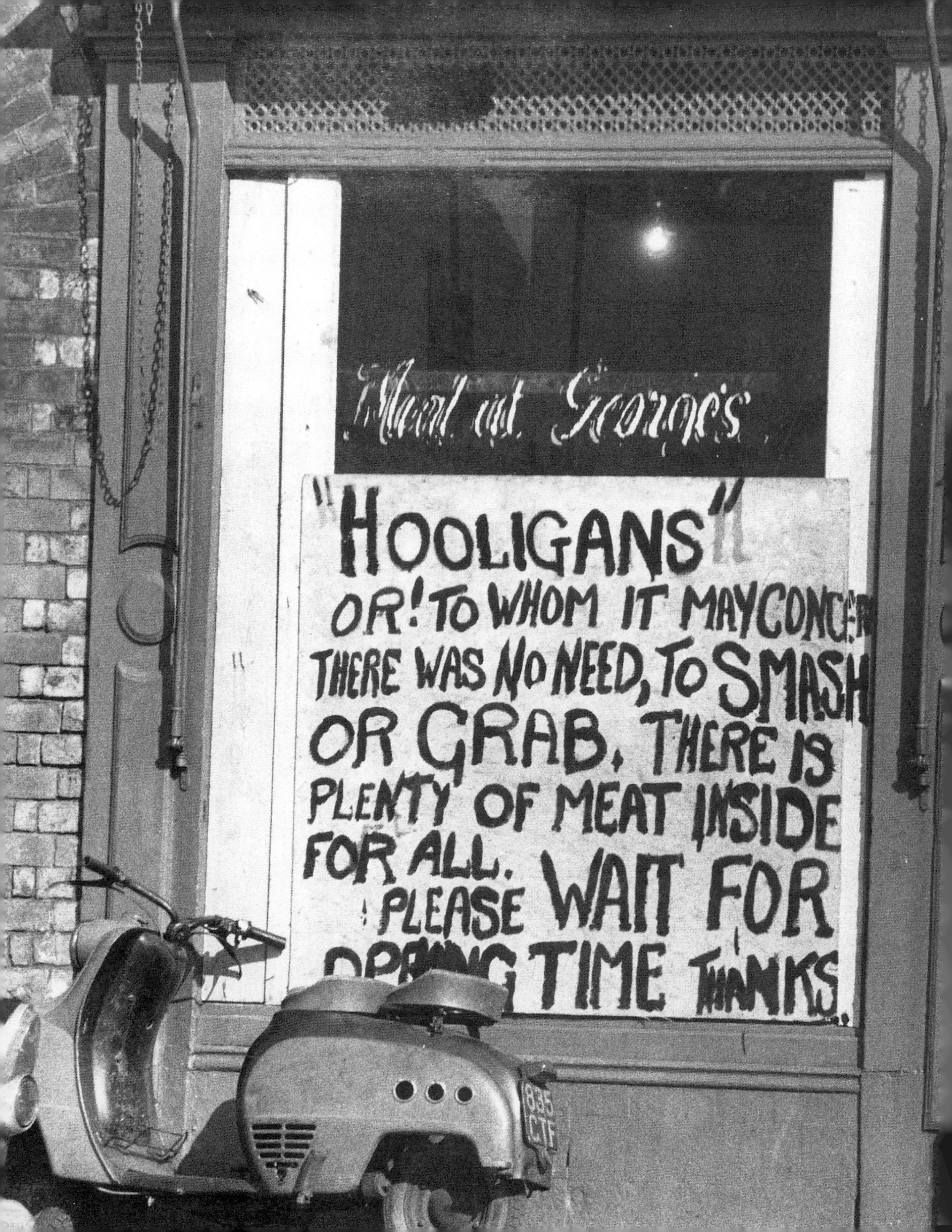
Meat at George's
"HOOLIGANS"
OR! TO WHOM IT MAY
THERE WAS NO NEED, TO SMASH
OR GRAB. THERE IS
PLENTY OF MEAT INSIDE
FOR ALL.
PLEASE WAIT FOR
TIME THANKS
835 CTF

Out of water, on with
NULON

MIRABEL ST.

JEROME ST.

dura-glit

THE WADDING WITH
THE BUILT-IN SHINE!

MAGIC WADDING
dura-glit

# List of images